WASHINGTON, D.C.

Carol M. Highsmith

CRESCENT BOOKS · NEW YORK

This 2000 edition is published by Crescent Books,
an imprint of Random House Value Publishing,
a division of Random House, Inc., New York.

Crescent is a registered trademark and the colophon
is a trademark of Random House, Inc.

Random House
New York • Toronto • London • Sydney • Auckland
www.randomhouse.com

Printed and bound in Singapore

Library of Congress Cataloging-in-Publication Data
Highsmith, Carol M., 1946–
Washington, D.C. / Carol M. Highsmith and Ted Landphair.
p.   cm.
ISBN 0-517-16235-0
1. Washington (D.C.)—Pictorial works. I. Landphair, Ted, 1942– II. Title.
F195.H52 2000
975.3—dc21   00-030336

8   7   6   5   4   3   2

_____

Project Editor: Donna Lee Lurker
Text written by Ted Landphair
Designed by Robert L. Wiser, Archetype Press, Inc., Washington, D.C.

All photographs by Carol M. Highsmith except for the White House Oval Office,
page 17, courtesy of the White House Historical Association.

WASHINGTON, D.C.: AN INTRODUCTION TO THE NATION'S CAPITAL

As visitors amble among the stirring monuments, superlative museums, and subtle neighborhoods of the nation's capital, they are savoring the inspirational fruits of lofty dreamers' labors. Mercurial French planner Pierre-Charles L'Enfant created a baroque Plan of the City in 1791 after slogging with George Washington through the malarial bogs near the tobacco wharves of Georgetown, Maryland. Washington picked this site, influenced by his own prosperity at nearby Mount Vernon and persuaded by the dandy location between the American North and South. L'Enfant began his sketch with two nodes: a brambly spot for a "President's House" (L'Enfant envisioned a palace) along an old footpath, and a loftier point for a "Congress House" atop a hill, a mile or so down that trail. Broad avenues spread outward in goosefoot fashion, piercing circles and squares. A "vast esplanade"—later the National Mall—was reserved for mansions and embassies. Vistas of the Potomac River, a grand canal, and the prime axes of government were meticulously calculated. Curiously, the aristocratic L'Enfant made no provision for the U.S. Supreme Court.

At first, L'Enfant's vision of a majestic monumental hub went largely unrealized. Tenements sprouted at the Capitol doorstep, and Pennsylvania Railroad tracks and coal piles besooted the "esplanade." So rough-and-tumble was the neighborhood that arose in the geographic slice between Pennsylvania Avenue and the City Canal that locals called it "Murder Bay." And the canal, fouled daily by Center Market butchers and fishmongers, devolved into an open sewer.

Congress determined to erase the embarrassing squalor with a swashbuckling beautification program, born in the Beaux-Arts "City Beautiful" swoon of the 1893 Chicago World's Columbian Exposition. The Senate's parks commission appointed the fair's mastermind, architect Daniel Burnham, to design another Great White City. This one would be permanent.

Burnham and the commissioners sailed off on a European pilgrimage. Their resulting 1901 Plan for Washington laid out new congressional buildings near the Capitol and refreshed the National Mall. Tree rows, carriage roads, and the lead elements in a parade of cultural museums replaced the railroad tracks and coal heaps. Dredgers drained the swamps beyond the Washington Monument with an eye toward a memorial to Abraham Lincoln. In "Swampoodle," a derelict immigrant neighborhood a block from the Capitol, Burnham himself created a mammoth Union Station that was inspired by Rome's majestic baths.

World War I interrupted the makeover, but a construction blitz, beginning with the Lincoln Memorial in 1922, was soon at hand. In a relative flash at the height of the Great Depression, contractors crammed the triangle between Pennsylvania Avenue and the new Constitution Avenue with gargantuan federal office and archives buildings, each with forbidding façades and red-tile roofs.

More than a generation later, a third great restoration plan took shape on the north side of Pennsylvania Avenue and spread outward. It began when President John F. Kennedy, in his inaugural ride up the avenue, took disdainful notice of what had happened to the city's commercial core. As cheap liquor stores, tawdry peep stalls, and boarded-up shops passed in review, the well-bred president is said to have barked to an aide, "It's a disgrace—fix it," or words to that effect.

And a remarkable public-private partnership did fix it. It rehabilitated historic office buildings, constructed luxury condominiums, sank a lush garden in the middle of Pennsylvania Avenue, and seeded a lively arts district that has since probed far into downtown. Preservationists literally saved the Willard "Hotel of Presidents" from the wrecker's ball. Georgetown boomed and power brokers gravitated to shining new K Street towers, commerce blossomed around each new Metro subway stop, and a sparkling arena near Chinatown and the refurbished "black Broadway" district coaxed life back into Washington nights. At last one of President Kennedy's favorite quotations, from Pericles' address to the Athenians, could again apply: "We do not imitate, for we are a model to others."

Then in 2000, the District of Columbia government announced still another ambitious plan for the nation's capital: up to three thousand new housing units and dozens of shops, museums, and theaters would be constructed in an already-vibrant "living downtown."

The upshot for Washington visitors is one of the world's astonishing shows—a dizzying array of free or inexpensive tourist options, too many for any one stay. There are numerous exhibits and sights to visit that include the original Declaration of Independence at the National Archives, the dozens of *incunabula*—works printed before 1500—at the Library of Congress, and watching where the buck starts at the Bureau of Engraving and Printing. Or one can just gambol amid the six thousand Japanese cherry trees in bloom each spring or fly a kite on the lawn between rows of Smithsonian museums.

Even with innumerable free activities from which to choose, visitors still manage to spend more than $6 billion each year in the Washington area. If they look hard enough as they wander the revitalized Capital of the Free World, they may see not only yesterday's plans in flower, but also today's dreamers hard at work.

In his 1791 plan for the new city of Washington, Frenchman Pierre-Charles L'Enfant envisioned a "vast esplanade" running westward from what he called the "Congress House." Along this idyllic promenade, L'Enfant foresaw embassies, splendid homes, an equestrian statue of George Washington, a grand canal fed by freshets from Tiber Creek, and "all such sort of places as may be attractive to the learned and afford diversion to the idle." Eventually the National Gallery of Art and buildings of the Smithsonian Institution lined the National Mall, an obelisk monument to Washington bisected it, and a memorial to President Abraham Lincoln anchored the opposite end. For a time, though, railroad tracks and coal piles fouled the Mall, and the "grand" canal was a sluggish open sewer.

The Washington Monument (right), which rises just over 555 feet above the city, took thirty-six years to complete. Construction of the gigantic obelisk, containing an estimated thirty-six thousand marble stones—including 192 contributed by states, nineteenth century organizations, and foreign governments—began in 1848. But attention to the task, as well as funding, were diverted by the U.S. Civil War and its aftermath. Finally, on December 6, 1884, the monument was topped by a marble capstone and a—then rare and expensive—nine-inch pyramid of cast aluminum. The Lincoln Memorial (opposite) was dedicated thirty-eight years later at the opposite end of a long reflecting pool that was part of a City Beautiful remake of the National Mall and adjacent Pennsylvania and Constitution Avenues.

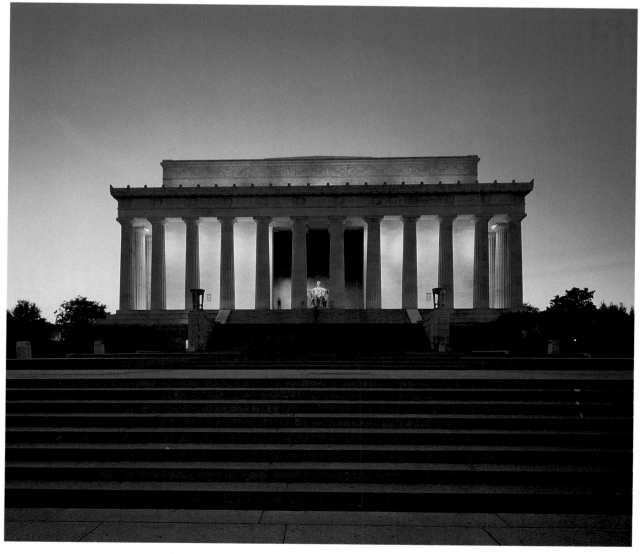

Dominating the Lincoln Memorial is Daniel Chester French's statue of the seated sixteenth president. It is made from twenty separate marble blocks that the sculptor seamlessly joined over thirteen years. Note the relaxed right hand and clenched left fist, suggesting Lincoln's gentle nature but steadfast determination to preserve the Union. Architect Henry Bacon's memorial that houses the statue is modeled after the Greek Parthenon. Its thirty-six Doric columns represent the states of the Union at the time of Lincoln's assassination in 1865; the names of the forty-eight states at the time of the memorial's completion in 1922 are inscribed along the building's frieze. The texts of Lincoln's Gettysburg and Second Inaugural addresses are carved into the memorial's marble walls.

Like Monticello, Thomas Jefferson's home in Virginia, the Jefferson Memorial, designed by architect John Russell Pope, is inspired by the Roman Pantheon. The memorial was erected along the Potomac River Tidal Basin between 1938 and 1943. Because of wartime metal shortages, however, Rudolph Evans's bronze statue of the third president was not completed and installed until four years later. The statue is encircled by Ionic columns and four panels containing excerpts from Jefferson's notable writings—including the 1776 Declaration of Independence. Each year in early spring, the Tidal Basin becomes the city's leading visitor attraction when successors to the original Yoshimo cherry trees, a gift from Japan in 1912, burst into delicate pink blossoms. Several small Japanese sculptures (lower left) dot the basin.

Monumental Washington is an "alabaster city" of federal memorials, museums, and office buildings that is quite different from the surrounding city neighborhoods. The McMillan Plan of the early twentieth century, inspired by the neoclassical Renaissance–style of the 1893 World's Columbian Exposition in Chicago, spruced up the seat of government by ousting tawdry pawn shops, barrooms, railroad stations, mills, and stables. Today, visitors from the world over come to absorb and photograph the grandeur of the nation's inspiring public buildings. Vistas are hard to come by, however, as Washington boasts only gentle hills. Many of the most alluring views are captured while landing at Washington's Reagan National Airport, or from vantage points across the river in Virginia.

George Washington selected the site of the "President's House" in swampy grounds down a brambly lane—later Pennsylvania Avenue— from the "Congress House." But Washington never lived there. In 1800, when the government was relocated to Washington from Philadelphia, John and Abigail Adams moved into the unfinished Georgian mansion, designed by Irishman James Hoban. Some accounts say the building acquired its white hue as painters sought to hide fire damage from the British burning of Washington during the War of 1812. Each Yuletide, the National Christmas Tree towers over the Ellipse behind the White House. Thomas Jefferson added an extension to the mansion that includes the Oval Office. But it was not until 1909 that a president—William Howard Taft—chose it to be his working office.

The "Old Executive Office Building" (far left) was built between 1871 and 1888 to hold three Cabinet departments. Designer Alfred Mullett later committed suicide in despair over the slow payment for his work. His French Second Empire–style creation, which Mark Twain judged "the ugliest building in America," does feature a stunning interior court (top left). Today the vice president and presidential staffers labor in its warrens. Blair House (center left) on Lafayette Square hosts visiting dignitaries. In 1951, armed Puerto Rican terrorists broke in and unsuccessfully attempted to reach President Harry Truman, who was living there during a White House renovation. Robert Mills's massive, classical Greek–style Treasury Building (lower left) was built on Pennsylvania Avenue in 1851, ruining Pierre L'Enfant's envisioned Capitol-to-White House vista.

The U.S. Capitol Building was the centerpiece of L'Enfant's Plan for Washington. The site L'Enfant chose for the building was atop Jenkins Hill, from which radiated broad avenues named for the original states. In 1793 William Thornton, a physician and amateur architect, won the competition to design the building, whose several stages would not be fully completed until 1960. George Washington laid the cornerstone of the "Congress House"—which, in its first phase, was an unremarkable building topped with a low dome—with a silver trowel that is still used for laying important public cornerstones. Only after the British burned the incomplete building and most of the volumes of the Library of Congress—then housed in the Capitol—in 1814 did construction of the central rotunda and towering dome begin.

Among the magnificent interior spaces in Washington is the Capitol Rotunda, 183 feet high and almost 96 feet across. It is topped by Constantino Brumidi's epic fresco, *The Apotheosis of Washington.* The artwork shows the first president attended by allegorical figures, including those representing the original thirteen states. Brumidi, who had worked on the Vatican, died while working on the frieze (center left) that encircles the rotunda 75 feet above the floor. John Trumbull, a onetime aide to General Washington, executed four of the paintings (lower left) at floor level where statues and busts, mostly of presidents, stand. More than twenty eminent individuals, including Pierre L'Enfant and presidents Lincoln and Kennedy, have lain in state in the Rotunda.

Clio, the Muse of History, stands inside Carlo Franzoni's marble sculpture, *Car of History* (top right), in the Capitol's Statuary Hall. She records events as they occur. It was once a whimsical congressional tradition to set the clock as far backward as necessary to complete the day's business. Statuary Hall (far right), which salutes notable former members, served as the House chamber until 1857. Portraits of former speakers of the House line the Speakers' Lobby (lower right). The original papers of President Andrew Jackson are among the artifacts on display in the Old Senate Chamber (center right). Jackson served in both the House and Senate before leading American forces against the British in the Battle of New Orleans during the War of 1812.

Founded in 1793, the Library of Congress is America's oldest national cultural institution—and the world's largest universal collection of thought and creativity. It is housed in three buildings: the grandiose Jefferson Building, a 1938 annex named for President John Adams, and a modern nine-story repository dedicated to President James Madison, built in the 1970s. The dome of the historic Jefferson Building is topped by a regilded Torch of Learning and stands beyond the Capitol's own dome on Capitol Hill (top left). The Capitol dome can be seen vividly from the Jefferson Building's north corridor windows (opposite). The Jefferson and Madison buildings are pictured lower left. In 1993, the LOC accepted its symbolic one hundred millionth acquisition, a collection of watercolors and pencil drawings.

The first great building of the Library of Congress was appropriately named after Thomas Jefferson. When the meager collection housed in Congress's "library apartment" at the Capitol was destroyed by the British in 1814, Jefferson restocked the collection with 6,487 works from his library. Many were in French and others were, at the time, deemed "too philosophical" by members of Congress. Philip Martiny's sculpture of a female figure holding a torch of knowledge (top right) stands at the foot of a grand staircase in the Jefferson Building's Great Hall. Only congressional members and esteemed researchers are admitted to the building's Members' Room (lower right). The Great Hall (far right), leading to the equally sumptuous Main Reading Room, accentuates the Library's reputation as a temple of knowledge.

Architect Cass Gilbert designed the United States Supreme Court Building, but only after Justice William Howard Taft, the only person to serve as both president and a High Court justice, persuaded Congress to construct a building to house the tribunal. Prior to 1935, the Court met at the Capitol and even in nearby taverns. On a pediment above the building's inscribed dedication to "Equal Justice Under the Law," allegorical icons (top left) to Liberty, Order, and Authority are joined by more modern figures. Beside the imposing stairway is James Earle Fraser's figure, *Contemplation of Justice* (center left). The Court's proceedings in its sumptuous chambers (lower left) are open to the public from the first Monday in October through late April.

Over the years, Pennsylvania Avenue, a little more than one mile in length in its ceremonial core between the Capitol and the White House—with an inconvenient dog-leg turn at the Treasury Building—has been a parade and funeral ground, grand shopping arcade and shabby urban disgrace, classical architectural laboratory, and line of demarcation between federal and city authority. And as these photographs (left) make clear, "America's Main Street" is also a place to frolic, to see and be seen, and to speak one's mind. During the Great Depression, massive Federal Triangle public buildings changed the face of Pennsylvania Avenue—wiping out unsavory neighborhoods like "Murder Bay"—and today the avenue is home to chic restaurants, elegant penthouse apartments, and restored theaters and hotels.

The nation's memorial to fallen police officers stands across from the National Building Museum (top right). Originally the Pension Building, this elaborate 1877 structure, designed by Army Quartermaster General Montgomery Meigs, held the staff that oversaw the pension benefits to Civil War veterans. Outside, its astonishing, twelve-hundred-foot-long terra cotta frieze depicts aspects of Civil War military life. As the National Building Museum, this monolith houses imaginative architectural and urban-design exhibits. Its Great Hall (opposite) is a favorite inaugural ball locale. The lines of Arthur Erickson's Canadian Chancery (lower left) complement those of I.M. Pei's East Wing of the National Gallery of Art across the street. Civil War photographer Mathew Brady once kept studios in what is now Sears House (lower right).

Architect John Russell Pope designed the National Archives Building, the largest structure among the procession of buff-colored limestone Federal Triangle buildings. They replaced seedy rooming houses, chop-suey joints, tattoo parlors, and dingy bars within the wedge between Pennsylvania and Constitution Avenues. Center Market, a thriving outdoor marketplace to which shoppers flocked by streetcar from 1801 to 1931, stood on the Archives Building site. Alongside Center Market, butchers routinely dumped rotted fish and poultry innards into the odiferous B Street Main, a remnant of the city's old City Canal that was eventually paved over to create Constitution Avenue. Inside the Archives Building are priceless treasures of American democracy, including the Declaration of Independence, U.S. Constitution (top left), and the Bill of Rights.

"Market Space," a row of dry-goods emporiums, department stores, lawyers' offices, and cigar dealers across from Center Market on Pennsylvania Avenue at the corner of Seventh Street, was once the vortex of Washington commerce. In the massive remaking of Pennsylvania Avenue in the 1980s under a public-private partnership, these businesses were swept away to build Market Square (top right), a development of 225 upscale housing units. Their residents enjoy the city's best view of the National Mall, including the National Gallery of Art's sculpture garden (lower right), which opened in 1999. Below Market Square at the U.S. Navy Memorial (opposite), a lone bronze seaman walks patrol atop a world map etched into a granite floor. Nearby is the U.S. Naval Heritage Center.

The $126-million FBI Building, which opened in 1974, was the most expensive project ever undertaken by the federal Public Buildings Service. The fortresslike structure was quickly lampooned by architectural critics—one called it the "Nightmare on Pennsylvania Avenue." Even FBI Director J. Edgar Hoover stuck a note in bureau files that read, "That's the goddamnedest ugliest building I've ever seen." But FBI Headquarters is a popular visitor attraction because of its engrossing tour, which covers everything from a stash of confiscated guns to a rogues' gallery of gangsters whose capture brought fame to Hoover and the bureau. Visitors get a peek, too, at the FBI crime laboratory that pioneered computerized fingerprinting, firearms matching, and suspect sketches, as well as DNA analysis.

Built in 1899 to house the main post office, the looming Romanesque-revival building along Pennsylvania Avenue survived many attempts to tear it down after the Post Office Department left in 1934. Now justifiably called the *Old* Post Office Building, it was once described by the *New York Times* as "a cross between a cathedral and a cotton mill." Those who venture up the open-air elevator to the 315-foot tower that holds its giant clock—whose hour hands measure seven feet long—get one of the best panoramic views of the capital city. Eventually tenants such as the National Endowment for the Arts occupied the upper floors, and the airy atrium was turned into a food court and indoor mall that is popular with tour-bus groups.

Washington's Federal Triangle complex of behemoth buildings proved to be a mixed blessing. Modeled after the Louvre and constructed under the doting eyes of Treasury Secretary Andrew Mellon and the city's Fine Arts commissioners, it replaced a shantytown, but its "Great Wall" of façades and army of bureaucrats who rushed from the buildings at workday's end drained the life out of Washington's old downtown. No one who found work building the Commerce, Justice, and other department headquarters complained, however, as it came in the throes of the Great Depression of the 1930s. Not just carpenters and masons got jobs; some of the nation's finest Depression artwork, created under the auspices of the Works Progress Administration, lines the halls of Triangle buildings.

Pennsylvania Avenue widens at one point into what was once a traffic island where a statue of Alexander "Boss" Shepherd stood. Shepherd was "governor" in the 1870s, when Washington was run like a distant territory. He spruced up the city but was ousted for corruption, and his statue was unceremoniously hauled off to a sewage plant. As urban renewal fever spread in the 1960s, President Richard Nixon's advisers unveiled plans to expand the modest traffic island into a colossal "National Square," *à la* Moscow's Red Square, by tearing down venerable buildings like the National Press Club. The plan was howled down, and National Square evolved into Freedom Plaza (opposite), now one of the city's favorite spots for colorful festivals.

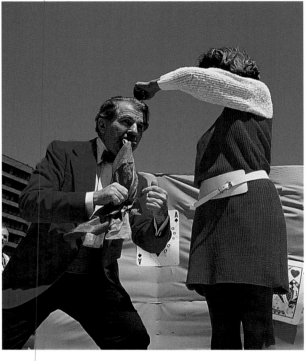

From the southeast corner of the Treasury Building grounds, the view down Pennsylvania Avenue (far right) has seen many changes in the past quarter century, including the wholesale renovation of the Willard Hotel in the foreground and the addition of new office buildings. History seems to repeat itself from time to time on the avenue as costumed characters recall the days when presidents and their entourages freely walked the city. At one event (top right), history buffs from the Society of Cincinnati celebrated the return of a monument to the hero of Gettysburg, Union General George Meade, to the grounds of a U.S. courthouse after fifteen years in storage. Elsewhere (center and lower right), members of the "Time Travelers" organization stroll the avenue.

In the middle of Pennsylvania Avenue is the astonishingly serene Pershing Park. Its greenery screens a dozen charms that include a waterfall, a small skating rink, and a granite tableau recalling General "Black Jack" Pershing's exploits. Pershing and twenty-five thousand of his soldiers marched up the avenue and under a temporary Arc de Triomphe at the close of World War I. Not far away, is the Bureau of Engraving and Printing (top left), a popular visitor attraction that cranks out billions of paper bills— and billions more postage stamps— each year. Relatively undiscovered is the National Academy of Sciences headquarters (lower left) on Constitution Avenue. Among its attractions are a Galileo door relief (center left) and a pendulum swinging from the building's fifty-six-foot domed ceiling.

A memorial amphi-theater near the Tomb of the Unknowns in the center of Arlington National Cemetery is the site of state funerals as well as annual Memorial Day and Veterans Day ceremonies. Every American president of the twentieth century presided over such gatherings. Arlington National Cemetery is located in northern Virginia, directly across Memorial Bridge from the Lincoln Memorial, on land once owned by George Washington Parke Custis, the adoptive grandson of George Washington, and later by Custis's daughter, Mary, and her husband, Robert E. Lee. The estate was named in honor of the Custis family's ancestral home in Virginia's Tidewater region. The visitor center at Arlington National Cemetery contains historical displays about the cemetery and its history, as well as a small gift shop.

The Custis-Lee mansion, or "Arlington House," overlooks the Arlington National Cemetery grounds. In 1861, with Robert E. Lee off commanding Virginia's Confederate forces, the mansion was seized by Union troops. A 210-acre section of the surrounding estate was set aside as a military cemetery, some say out of hatred for Lee by Union Quartermaster General Montgomery Meigs, who had lost a son in battle. Following the Civil War, the cemetery's superintendent lived and worked in Arlington House. In 1933 it was transferred to the National Park Service, which gradually refurbished the manse. In 1955 the residence was designated a memorial to Robert E. Lee, and some original and many period furnishings have since been obtained to restore its antebellum flavor.

Felix de Weldon completed the world's largest bronze sculpture, the Iwo Jima Memorial (opposite)—properly, the Marine Corps War Memorial—in 1954 and placed it at Arlington National Cemetery. It was inspired by Associated Press photographer Joe Rosenthal's image of five marines and one Navy corpsman raising the American flag atop Mount Suribachi during World War II. Queen Juliana of the Netherlands presented the adjacent bell tower, now called the Netherlands Carillon (lower left), in appreciation for U.S. support during the war. Other designated memorials at Arlington include those to the "Rough Riders" (top left), women in military service (top right), Americans who lost their lives at sea (center left), unknowns from several wars (center right), and Navy "Seabees" (lower right).

Arlington National
Cemetery has more
than doubled in size
since the U.S. Civil
War. The first person
interred was a Confed-
erate soldier who had
died in captivity. Many
of the five thousand
original gravesites were
crude affairs, as at first
only unidentified
soldiers or those whose
families were too poor
to retrieve the remains
of their loved ones were
buried at Arlington—
their gravesites noted
with wooden markers.
Today more than
two hundred and fifty
thousand veterans,
including presidents
Taft and Kennedy,
prizefighter Joe Louis,
and orator William
Jennings Bryan—
and some family
members—lie in
Arlington National
Cemetery. Also
entombed there are
astronaut Virgil
"Gus" Grissom and
the remains of the
seven Challenger crew
members. Flags (far
right) are permitted
at gravesites only
during the Memorial
Day weekend.

Arlington National Cemetery is not the only prominent final resting place in the Washington area. Two U.S. Supreme Court justices are buried at Rock Creek Cemetery, where, in 1890, Henry Adams commissioned sculptor Augustus Saint-Gaudens to create a monument (opposite) to his dead wife. First Lady Eleanor Roosevelt often visited the statue, called *Grief*, which critic Alexander Wolcott deemed "the most beautiful thing ever fashioned by the hand of man on this continent." One of the city's oldest African-American church cemeteries is Mount Zion (above left) in Georgetown. The capital's oldest grave-yard is Congressional Cemetery (lower left), where photog-rapher Mathew Brady, Vice President Elbridge Gerry— who devised "gerry-mandering"—march king John Philip Sousa, and FBI Director J. Edgar Hoover (lower right) are buried.

Lafayette Square across from the White House has been a traditional assembly ground for political protest. It honors the Marquis de Lafayette's triumphant return to the United States in 1824. Clark Mills's equestrian statue of Andrew Jackson (top right)—which he duplicated in Nashville and New Orleans—dominates the park. Henry Ellicott's figure of Union General Winfield Scott Hancock rides tall (lower left) on Pennsylvania Avenue. More than two hundred thousand African-American troops who served the Union during the Civil War are honored (lower right) in Ed Hamilton's statue in the city's Cardozo section. Union Cavalry general Philip Sheridan's likeness (opposite), by Gutzon Borglum—the tempermental sculptor of Mount Rushmore—towers above the Embassy Row circle that bears Sheridan's name.

Not until 1995, four decades after the Korean War, did Americans and their United Nations allies receive a memorial to their service in that distant, sometimes forgotten, conflict. Much of the $18 million raised to build the Korean War Veterans Memorial in a grove on the National Mall came from veterans themselves and from donations from Korean corporations operating in the United States. The memorial's striking elements include Frank Gaylord's nineteen stainless-steel troopers patrolling through juniper bushes and granite rows that suggest Korea's tilled terrain; and Louis Nelson's polished granite wall—on which are etched the visages of thousands of support personnel, from pilots to M.A.S.H. medical corpsmen. "Freedom," reads one inscription at the memorial, "is not free."

The volume of sentimental objects left at the Vietnam Veterans Memorial (right) has lessened over the years, but the National Park Service is still collecting dog tags, teddy bears, poems, flowers, and more. And visitors are still apt to see a loved one tracing a name from "the Wall." There are actually two polished granite walls, each 246.8 feet long, meeting at a 125-degree angle to form an open wedge. Maya Lin, a Yale University architecture student, designed the memorial that was completed in 1982. Two statue groupings— including Glenna Goodacre's tribute to women who served as nurses in Southeast Asia (opposite)—have since been added to the site in Constitution Gardens on the National Mall. Approximately fifty-eight thousand names are etched into "the Wall."

It was almost twenty years after Franklin Delano Roosevelt's death before the nation's longest-serving president was remembered with a memorial—a humble block of Vermont marble on the National Archives Building lawn. Its simplicity respected Roosevelt's own wishes, expressed to Justice Felix Frankfurter in 1941, but public sentiment for a grander memorial eventually prevailed. In the mid-1990s, landscape architect Lawrence Halprin's tribute to F.D.R., complete with a waterfall (center left) and a "touching wall" for the visually impaired (lower right), rose in West Potomac Park. Inside four open-air "rooms" are several statues, including those of Roosevelt himself (top left), an Appalachian couple (top right), a figure listening to a "fireside chat" (center right), and men in a bread line (lower left).

69

In 1942, Michael Lantz carved the limestone sculpture *Man Controlling Trade* (far left) on site outside the Federal Trade Commission's headquarters at the apex of the Federal Triangle. A lion (top left) is one element of architect David Buckley's National Law Enforcement Officers Memorial at Judiciary Square. Robert Berks unveiled his approachable statue of Albert Einstein (center left) in the courtyard of the National Academy of Sciences in 1979. A year later, J. Seward Johnson mounted his bizarre, five-piece aluminum sculpture, *The Awakening* (lower left), at Hains Point. The spot is named for Peter Hains, an army engineer who in the 1890s supervised a flood-control project on the Potomac River that created the Tidal Basin and a landfill site on which the Lincoln Memorial would be built.

The scientific empire that became the Smithsonian Institution began in 1849 in this Norman-style "castle" designed by James Renwick Jr., after whom the Smithsonian's Renwick Gallery of design and crafts is named. The Smithsonian owes its beginnings to James Smithson, a wealthy English scientist who never visited the United States. He left half a million dollars—a fortune in 1829—to found, specifically in Washington, "an Establishment for the increase and diffusion of knowledge of men." It took the better part of two more decades for Congress to agree to Smithson's wishes and to establish a governing board. Today the Smithsonian is an independent membership organization with multiple museums and galleries whose scholars conduct research and mount scientific expeditions around the world.

James Renwick Jr. built his Smithsonian Castle (top and center left) out of local sandstone. The building housed all facets of the operation—administration, laboratories, lecture halls, and art galleries. The Smithsonian secretary and his family even lived there. Today the Castle is the information hub for visitors. The Arts and Industries Building (opposite and center right) was first used for President James Garfield's inaugural ball in 1881. Exhibitions, enriched by the receipt of giant steam-powered pumps, presses, engines, and other technical wonders from the Philadelphia Centennial of 1876, followed. Seasonally rotated gardens (lower left) include a rooftop parterre named for donor Enid A. Haupt. The Smithsonian Natural History Museum (lower right) was the first to locate across the Mall.

In many cities a clock or department store doorway is a favorite meeting spot. In Washington, the stuffed African bush elephant—the largest ever recorded—inside the Smithsonian's 1910 National Museum of Natural History has been a place where families and friends, dispersed among the Mall's many attractions, traditionally get reconnected. Dinosaur bones (top left), gems, anthropological displays, and even an insect zoo are among the other exhibits. The National Museum of American History, opened in 1964, has its longtime-favorite exhibits including First Ladies' gowns (lower left) and the original Star-Spangled Banner. It is also the repository of everyday American artifacts such as clocks, bicycles, washing machines, and even the Woolworth's lunch counter (center left) where a sit-in was organized in the 1960s.

Ever since it opened during the 1976 U.S. Bicentennial, the Smithsonian's Air and Space Museum has ranked at or near the top of Washington tourist destinations. Along with its displays of rocketry, space exploration (opposite), and futuristic travel, some of its most popular exhibits have been the oldest. They include the Wright Brothers' flyer (top right) flown in man's first controlled and sustained flight at Kitty Hawk, North Carolina, in 1903; and the *Spirit of St. Louis,* the craft that Charles Lindbergh flew solo, nonstop across the Atlantic in 1927. Favorites, too, are IMAX theater presentations on a screen five stories high that challenge the imagination and the senses. Like other Smithsonian museums, Air and Space has a renowned research library.

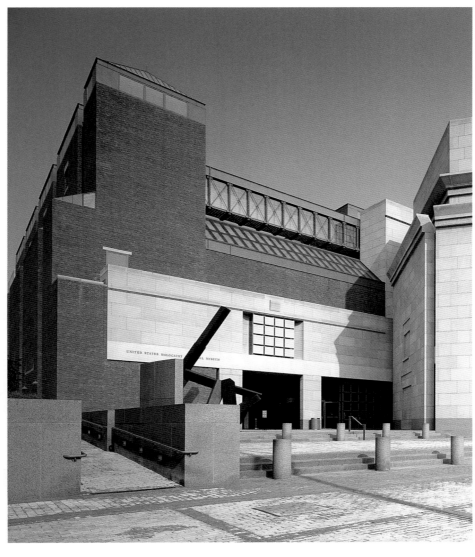

A remarkable, sometimes disturbing, addition to the Washington museum scene in 1993 was the U.S. Holocaust Memorial Museum (top left) on Independence Avenue at the National Mall. Names (lower left) and photographic portraits (far left) of victims of Nazi terror in Europe are some of the least graphic exhibits. Architect James Freed incorporated elements of concentration camps and gas chambers and other symbols of the persecution of millions of Jews, Gypsies, homosexuals, dissidents, and others. Each visitor receives an identity card of a victim of the same sex and approximate age, containing background on the person's life and death. The museum also makes its database available to Holocaust survivors and descendants to help them trace the fate of friends and relatives.

At the 1997 Newseum (top right) in Arlington, visitors can explore the diversity and impact of modern mass media—even taking turns delivering the news before a camera. The Smithsonian's National Postal Museum (lower left and lower right), located in the mammoth former Washington city post office next to Union Station on Capitol Hill, tells the story of the nation's mail service and displays stamps, postcards, and other philatelic objects from a collection that numbers in the millions. The Capital Children's Museum (opposite), also near Union Station, opened in 1979 as the city's most interactive museum. Youngsters can "drive" a bus, appear in a Bugs Bunny or Daffy Duck cartoon, slide down a fire pole, and giggle their way through a maze.

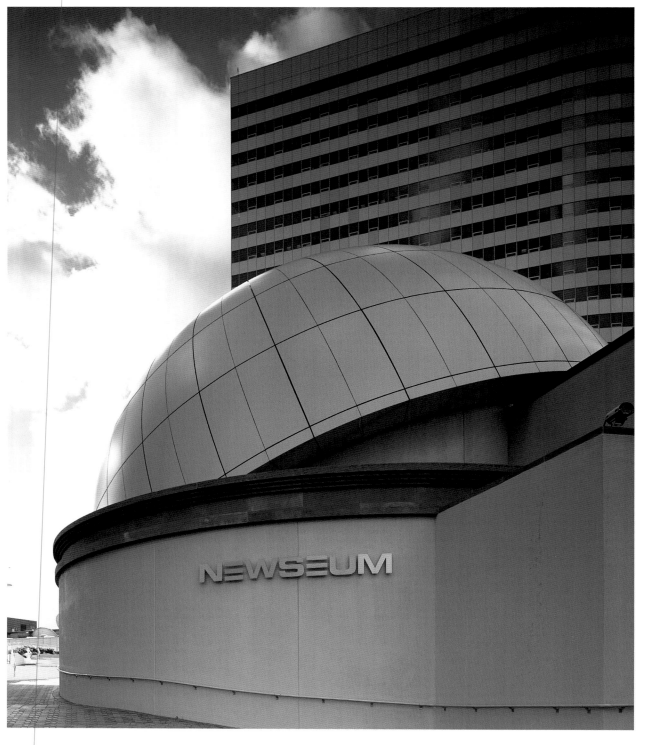

The Smithsonian Institution's Renwick Gallery (far left and top left), Washington's first sizable art museum, was designed by James Renwick Jr. to hold the collection of William Corcoran. In 1897 Corcoran's holdings moved to larger quarters, and the building was transformed into a courthouse. Returned to Smithsonian ownership in 1966, it was named for Renwick and restored as a gallery of French Renaissance art. The collection of the National Museum of American Art (center left) also moved from the National Mall to Gallery Place near Chinatown. It features the world's largest assemblage of American artwork including folk art. Renoir's *Luncheon of the Boating Party* (lower left) is a prize possession of the Phillips Collection, America's oldest museum of modern art, near Dupont Circle.

The National Gallery of Art consigns its modern-art collection to a fittingly stark East Wing (far right and top right), which displaced a tennis court and 120 climbing rose bushes. Andrew Mellon, benefactor of the original National Gallery in 1941, had purchased enough land for a later expansion. The 1978 East Building, whose trapezoidal footprint matches the unusual site where Pennsylvania Avenue, the National Mall, and Capitol Hill converge, was designed by Gold Medal architect I. M. Pei. It often houses smash visiting exhibitions, modernist or not. In 1999 the National Gallery used still more of its reserved land for a new sculpture garden to display its modern-art statuary (center right and lower right). Each winter, its fountain becomes a popular ice rink.

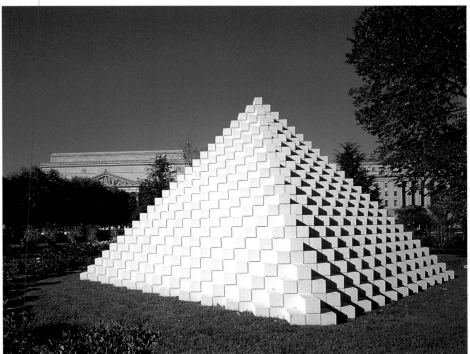

The Smithsonian Institution has a modern-art collection of its own that is housed in and around the Hirshhorn Museum building on the National Mall. Architect Gordon Bunshaft designed the 1974 drum-shaped granite-aggregate and concrete building that is elevated on four gigantic piers. The avant-garde museum, which traces the roots of modernism to the early eighteenth century, is named for Latvian-born Joseph H. Hirshhorn, whose 1966 bequest of twelve thousand works of modern art formed the bulk of the collection. The building of four stories and a balcony overlooking the Mall features an open inner core. The Hirshhorn's multi-terraced sculpture garden, with its own reflecting pool, lies several feet below the Mall. Each year, the Hirshhorn produces an eagerly anticipated film series.

The Smithsonian Institution includes specialized art galleries such as the National Museum of African Art (top left); the Arthur M. Sackler Gallery (top right and center left), which features Asian art; and the Freer Gallery of Art (center right), which displays unique collections like the works of James McNeill Whistler. A sentinel lion (lower left) guards the Corcoran Museum of Art, the city's largest independent art museum. The Corcoran is especially praised for its collection of European masters. The National Jewish Museum (lower right), on the ground floor of B'nai B'rith's International Headquarters, displays a range of art depicting Jewish culture and history. The Organization of American States offers a fine contemporary art collection, starting with a statue of Queen Isabella of Spain (opposite).

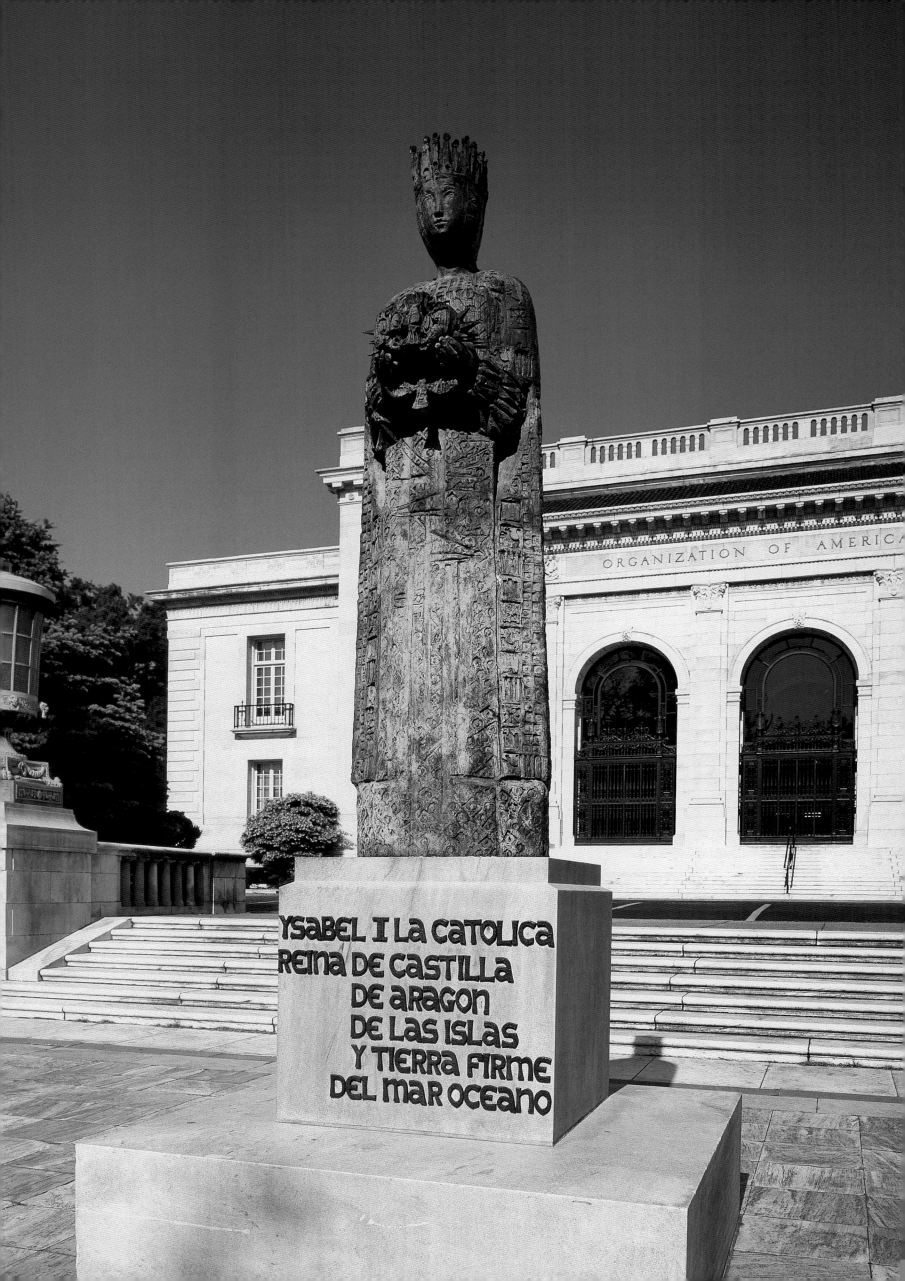

YSABEL I LA CATOLICA
REINA DE CASTILLA
DE ARAGON
DE LAS ISLAS
Y TIERRA FIRME
DEL MAR OCEANO

ORGANIZATION OF AMERICA

After the assassination of President Abraham Lincoln at Ford's Theater in 1865, outrage ran so deep that its owner was forced to close down. The facility was converted into government offices where, in 1893, twenty-two clerks were killed when a floor collapsed. The building has held a Lincoln assassination exhibit since 1932, but only after restoration and reopening of the theater (top left) by the National Park Service in 1968 were a tour and carefully researched exhibit (lower left) put in place. The latter includes a careful re-creation of the president's box (center left) and a display of artifacts taken from Lincoln's body (opposite). Visitors also tour the Petersen House across the street (top right and center right) where Lincoln died.

Constitution Hall (top right), owned by the Daughters of the American Revolution, is Washington's largest auditorium. The limestone building, designed by John Russell Pope—creator of the Jefferson Memorial, National Archives Building, and main wing of the National Gallery of Art—opened in 1929. Edward Durrell Stone's John F. Kennedy Center for the Performing Arts rose along the Potomac River on an old brewery site in 1971. Robert Berks's bust of President Kennedy in the Grand Foyer (center right) weighs three thousand pounds. In northern Virginia, Wolf Trap Farm Park (lower right), America's national park for the performing arts, attracts a panoply of performers. Farther into the Virginia countryside, the Central Intelligence Agency disdains public visits, but it has decorated "Company" headquarters with a courtyard display of secret codes (far right) etched into a waving metal sculpture.

The arching stone bridges and 1,750 acres of woodlands of Rock Creek Park (lower left and far left) stretch from Georgetown into Maryland. The area was spared from development when the federal government created one of the first national parks in 1890. There much earlier, at Fort Stevens, Confederate skirmishers had reached the capital city but were repulsed. Rock Creek Park is laced with twenty-nine miles of hiking paths and ten miles of equestrian trails, but automobile commuters often clog its winding roadway. The park features a nature center, amphitheater, golf course, tournament-quality tennis courts, and the National Zoo (top left and center left), which is a branch of the Smithsonian Institution. Washington's zoo was one of the nation's first to receive giant pandas from China.

The original Corinthian columns removed from the U.S. Capitol during 1957 renovations form an imposing peristyle at the 446-acre U.S. National Arboretum, the U.S. Agriculture Department's research and education facility. The columns languished in a lot for a quarter century until landscape designer Russell Page hit upon the idea of creating an "acropolis" at the arboretum. With financing from benefactor Ethel Garrett and approval from Congress, Page created a portico of columns, reclaimed Capitol stones, and a water stair. The National Arboretum is home to the National Bonsai Garden and the nation's official collection of herbs. The latter, containing more than eight hundred varieties, is the world's largest. The arboretum's gardens also show off boxwoods, dogwoods, azaleas, and historic rose displays.

Golfers at West Potomac Park (opposite) near the Jefferson Memorial enjoy spectacular views of majestic monuments. The U.S. Botanic Garden (top left), a stone's throw from the U.S. Capitol on the National Mall, got a wholesale renovation at the turn of the twenty-first century. Ever-captivating is its outdoor Bartholdi Park (top right). Along the Anacostia River shoreline, Kenilworth Gardens (center left) may be the world's only national park devoted to water plants. Kayaking is a favorite pastime on the Potomac River (center right). It flows under Arlington Memorial Bridge (lower left and lower right), which was built in 1932 to symbolically connect the North and South—specifically the memorial to President Lincoln with the former estate of Confederate commander Robert E. Lee.

The Potomac River
turns impassable in
the Great Falls rapids
(top right), upriver
from Washington. That
is why speculators built
the Chesapeake and
Ohio Canal alongside
the river to pierce the
western frontier. Spout
Run (lower left) is best
known to Washingtoni-
ans as an exit into civi-
lization off the bucolic
George Washington
Memorial Parkway.
A footpath off that
parkway (lower right)
reaches Theodore Roo-
sevelt Island in the
middle of the Potomac
River. Now a nature
preserve, it has been
home to Union Civil
War encampments,
a gun club, and lacrosse
fields. An antique,
hand-painted Dentzel
carousel (opposite) is a
delight at the National
Park Service's Glen
Echo Park, on the site
of an old Chautauqua
meeting ground
just over the state line
in Maryland.

Not just government business gets done in the nation's capital. Franklin Square (far left) provides a respite from work on K Street, the new heart of commercial Washington. K Street has become synonymous with Washington's most powerful law firms and influential lobbying organizations. Farragut Square (top left), named for Union Admiral David Farragut, sits directly on K in front of the prestigious Army-Navy Club. A grand cruciform (center left), with its precast aluminum clock inside the office building at 1001 Pennsylvania Avenue, attracted producers for the movie *Broadcast News*. They shot much of the 1987 comedy inside the building. The John Akridge Company's Homer Building (lower left) changed the face of a deteriorating neighborhood around what became "Metro Center," where three subway lines converge.

For a century it seemed everyone who was anyone stayed at the Willard Hotel—the "Hotel of Presidents"—on Pennsylvania Avenue. Julia Ward Howe wrote the words to "The Battle Hymn of the Republic" there. Ulysses S. Grant greeted supplicants in the lobby, which inspired the term "lobbying." Calvin Coolidge resided there during his entire vice presidency. But the Willard turned shabby after World War II and was closed for demolition in 1969. Saved after a remarkable preservationist campaign, it and its splendid lobby (center left), concierge desk (lower left), dining room (center right), and "Peacock Alley" hallway (lower right) were restored. One of the best views of the Washington Monument (opposite) could again be accessed from a window in the Willard's mansard roof.

Some of Washington's most prominent citizens keep apartments at the Watergate (far right). The building, just up the Potomac River from the John F. Kennedy Center for the Performing Arts, will long be synonymous in American history with the 1972 break-in of Democratic National Committee Headquarters that led to President Richard Nixon's resignation two years later. The burglars kept the Watergate (top right) in view from a much less pricey hotel across the street. Georgetown Park (center right), in the heart of a popular shopping and strolling neighborhood, is one of Washington's most stylish arcades. The Fashion Centre (lower right) at Pentagon City serves a sleek neighborhood of parks and high-rise office and apartment buildings near the world's most famous five-sided structure.

Washington's 1903 Union Station (top left) was a Beaux Arts transportation palace. It was the masterpiece of architect Daniel Burnham, majordomo of the 1893 Chicago World's Exposition. Like the Chicago fair, Lorado Taft's 1912 statue and fountain (top right) on Union Station's plaza honored Christopher Columbus. The terminal's grand presidential suite is now a fine dining room (center left) with exquisite detailing (lower left and right) by master restoration specialists. The East Hall (center right), which once held its own white-tablecloth restaurant, is now a chic shopping arcade. Union Station's West Hall (opposite) was the ticketing and baggage-check alcove. Older Washingtonians will not soon forget the years when the station turned tawdry and leaky and housed an ill-fated "National Visitor Center."

Arlington's Crystal City complex along the Potomac River offers spectacular views of Reagan National Airport and monumental Washington. The U.S. Navy, giant defense contractor McDonnell Douglas Corporation, and an array of high-tech research and consulting firms are among the tenants in millions of square feet of office space here. The complex, which has won several national architecture and landscape awards, also includes an enclosed shopping mall, health clubs, several hotels, and more than thirty-two hundred condominiums and apartments. The Arlington Symphony Orchestra holds concerts in an amphitheater, and residents enjoy a 1.5-acre water park, sixteen smaller parks, extensive public art—including interior tapestries and murals—and a climate-controlled pedestrian concourse that connects to a shopping mall and Metro station.

The nation's capital enjoys superb public transit and airline service. In 1998, Congress honored former president Ronald Reagan by renaming convenient Washington National Airport—just across the Potomac River—in his honor. A wholesale renovation of the historic terminal (opposite) was in progress at the time. Out in the Virginia countryside, an earlier futuristic concourse (top left), designed by Eero Saarinen and named for former secretary of state John Foster Dulles, opened in 1962. By the turn of the century Dulles had become the nation's fastest-growing airport, and Maryland's bustling BWI airport lies just as close to Washington. "Metro" light-rail lines (lower left) reach outward like an octopus into the suburbs from underground downtown stations. The system is among the world's safest and cleanest.

Georgetown University (far left), founded in 1789, is America's oldest Catholic university. Its hilltop tower can be seen for miles along the Potomac River. American University (top left), established in 1893, is the nation's only university to be chartered by Congress. During both world wars, the U.S. military took over much of the campus on Nebraska Avenue. In 1912, George Washington University (center left)—once called "Columbian University"—relocated to "Foggy Bottom," west of the White House on Pennsylvania Avenue. It is a neighborhood of Federal-style row houses—many of which the university occupied. Pope Leo XIII chartered the Catholic University of America (lower left) in 1887. In addition to its secular curriculum, the university grants degrees in theology and canon law.

117

Howard University (top right), founded in 1867, initially trained preachers to serve freed slaves. The academically rigorous, primarily African-American university is named for Union General Oliver O. Howard, who directed the Freedmen's Bureau. Howard's divinity school (opposite), designed by Charles Oakley, dates to 1870 when it was a Franciscan seminary. The Charles Sumner School (lower left) graduated the city's first black high-school class in 1877. The restored school, which was named for Senator Charles Sumner of Massachusetts, a tireless abolitionist, is now the museum and archive of Washington's public schools. Once a classroom-dormitory at the "National Deaf-Mute College," Gallaudet University's administration building (lower right) opened in 1877. Originally all-male, the school was named for its first president, Edward Miner Gallaudet.

The landmark that became Thomas Circle was one of many circles and squares laid out by Pierre L'Enfant along the diagonals of his original Plan for Washington. But the area, north of the White House where four important streets intersect, was relatively undeveloped until the Society of the Cumberland dedicated a statue there to Union General George Thomas in 1879. The event coincided with the city's first large-scale demonstration of electric lighting. The widening of Massachusetts Avenue and construction of its tunnel under Thomas Circle in 1940 helped change the neighborhood's character from residential to commercial. To the left is John Russell Pope's colonialstyle National City Christian Church; to the right, Judson York's Gothic Luther Place Memorial Church.

George Washington and Robert E. Lee worshipped at Alexandria's 1773 Christ Church (far left). Here, Lee was offered command of Virginia forces at the beginning of the Civil War. John Russell Pope's Temple of the Scottish Rite (top left), built for Washington's Masons in 1911, is modeled after the Mausoleum of Halicarnassus, one of the ancient world's Seven Wonders, in what is now Turkey. The Islamic Center (center left) is American Muslims' religious home. Its limestone façade, which complements the embassies and private mansions that surround it on Massachusetts Avenue, dutifully faces Mecca. The illuminated tower of the Temple of the Church of Jesus Christ of Latter-Day Saints, topped by the Mormon angel Moroni (lower left), is a familiar sight along the Capital Beltway in suburban Maryland.

The Byzantine-style Basilica of the National Shrine of the Immaculate Conception, on the grounds of Catholic University, is the Western Hemisphere's largest—and world's eighth-most spacious—house of worship. Bishop Thomas J. Shahan, the university's rector, returned from Rome in 1913 with Pope Pius X's support for building a shrine to the Virgin Mary. Bishop Shahan described his vision as a "hymn in stone." Not until 1959 was the upper church, replete with marble and mosaics, completed and dedicated. The shrine can accommodate up to six thousand worshipers. Each of its sixty chapels and oratories represents a story from the history of the Catholic Church. The shrine's 329-foot Knights' Tower was a gift of the Knights of Columbus.

The Washington National Cathedral, atop the city's highest point at Mount Saint Alban, soars higher than the Washington Monument. The architecture of this Protestant Episcopal cathedral—formally known as the Cathedral Church of Saint Peter and Saint Paul—was supervised by Philip Hubert Frohman for fifty-one years into 1971. The enormous cathedral, whose memorial, thanksgiving, and interfaith services have fulfilled Pierre L'Enfant's vision of a great "church for national purpose . . . equally open to all," was dedicated in 1907 by President Theodore Roosevelt, who exclaimed, "God speed the work!" No such thing happened, however. The Gothic cathedral remained in one stage of construction or another, down to the last gargoyle, for the next eighty-three years.

The Chesapeake and Ohio Canal operated along 184.5 miles of the Potomac River from Washington to Cumberland, Maryland, from 1828 to 1924, primarily hauling coal from western Maryland. Its aqueduct was Washington's first public water system. The canal included a tunnel wide enough for one boat at a time. A flood in 1899 and competition from the B&O Railroad ruined the enterprise. Years later, there was talk of filling in the canal and making it a highway. Instead, U.S. Supreme Court Justice William O. Douglas, an avid outdoorsman, led the successful fight to designate its entire length a national historical park. Today, millions of people enjoy hikes and bike rides along the towpath, as well as mule-drawn boat rides from Georgetown to Great Falls.

Georgetown was a thriving port long before there was a Washington to subsume it. Named for King George II—father of the sovereign whose tyrannical rule ignited the Revolutionary War—Georgetown remained an aloof but character-filled enclave. Until wholesale gentrification in the 1960s, Georgetown was a commercially and ethnically diverse—even dowdy—neighborhood. Today its Federal-style town-houses, multiple churches, fashionable shops, and trendy bars are much in style. Among its daytime diversions for visitors: taking a boat ride through locks on the Chesapeake and Ohio Canal (center left); touring the 1766 Old Stone House (center right)—once a residence and cabinet-maker's shop that is Washington's oldest-known surviving building; and shopping or dining at Washington Harbour, which replaced worn-out industrial buildings.

William Thornton, who worked on the U.S. Capitol, designed Tudor Place (top right) in Georgetown for a granddaughter of George and Martha Washington. The stucco façade and temple-style portico of the 1816 residence broke with colonial fashion. Robert Woods Bliss, heir to a patent-medicine fortune, and his wife Mildred bought and began improving an estate home called Dumbarton Oaks in 1920. They turned the manor (lower right) and grounds (opposite) into a must-see attraction. When the Blisses moved to California in 1940, they gave most of the estate to Harvard University, which has maintained the house as a center of Byzantine studies. The gardens, designed by Beatrix Jones Farrand and open to the public, remain a tranquil oasis in a frenetic capital city.

George Washington is revered as a general in the French and Indian War and the Revolutionary War, as the chairman of the 1787 Constitutional Convention, and as the nation's first president. Mount Vernon, his Virginia homestead atop a Potomac River bluff—built in 1743 by his half-brother, Lawrence—recalls George's days as a gentleman farmer. Here, two hundred slaves helped the family harvest maize and wheat, raise dairy cows, and spin cotton and wool. When Washington died, he owned ninety thousand acres in Virginia and another forty thousand in what is now West Virginia. America's preservationist movement can be traced to the purchase and restoration of the Mount Vernon Estate, which had fallen into ruin, by the Mount Vernon Ladies' Association in 1860.

George Washington enjoyed his home at Mount Vernon. But he most loved his land and gardens (far left), which the estate meticulously maintains to this day. As a surveyor, Washington helped lay out Alexandria (top left and lower left), which, like Georgetown, was a thriving Potomac River port. Wealthy planters gathered for trade and talk at its docks, where the primary product was tobacco from Virginia's "Northern Neck" between the Potomac and Rappahannock rivers. Old Town Alexandria, which has retained some of its original cobblestone streets and even an apothecary shop that was founded in 1792, was incorporated into the original District of Columbia, but was retroceded to Virginia in 1846. Whereas Georgetown's elite built mostly Federal-style townhouses, Georgian was the vogue in Alexandria.

Clara Barton, who had founded the American Red Cross out of her home in Dansville, New York, first used a house in the new development of Glen Echo, Maryland, as storage for Red Cross equipment while she lived nearby in the District of Columbia. In 1897 she moved thirty wagonloads of supplies—as well as staff members, volunteers, and herself—into the Glen Echo house, which she continued to use as both a home and a warehouse for disaster-relief supplies until she resigned from the Red Cross in 1904. The house is modeled after several that the Red Cross helped build in Johnstown, Pennsylvania, following the deadly 1899 flood. The National Park Service has restored several of its rooms.

After the Civil War, Frederick Douglass—himself a former slave and fiery abolitionist—ran the Freedman's Savings Bank. He lived and wrote in a fine Victorian home on a hilltop in Washington's Anacostia section, across what was once called the Eastern Branch of the Potomac River. Douglass had written a narrative of his life as a slave on a Maryland plantation and recruited African-American soldiers for Union regiments. He "broke the color line" when he bought the Anacostia house in 1877, naming it Cedar Hill and expanding it from fourteen to twenty-two rooms. Douglass spent his last year as U.S. minister to Haiti. His house, whose grounds offer a spectacular view of national monuments across the Anacostia River, is a National Historic Site.

In 1921, what is now called the Woodrow Wilson House (top left) was a surprise present by the former president to his second wife, Edith Bolling Wilson, who had assumed many chief executive's duties as "secret president" after Wilson suffered a stroke during his second term. Following a Scottish tradition, Wilson presented his wife with a key and piece of sod from what would become a magnificent garden (far left). After the president's death in 1924, Mrs. Wilson continued to enjoy the parlor (center left), music room (lower left), and garden until her own death in 1961. She bequeathed the house to the National Trust for Historic Preservation, which maintains it as "a unique time capsule of Washington history in the 1920s."

Capitol Hill (top right and far right), a neighborhood of classic row houses, corner food stores, ethnic restaurants, and surprisingly few retail shops and taverns, is "hot" real estate. The *Guide to the Architecture of Washington, D.C.,* by the American Institute of Architects, calls Capitol Hill "a favored enclave of that unique Washington type, the bohemian bureaucrat." Not surprisingly, many members of Congress and their staffs keep townhouses on the Hill. Just off East Capitol Street, opposite an emancipation monument, stands Robert Berks's statue of Mary McLeod Bethune and her young friends (center right). Bethune founded the National Council of Negro Women. Low-income dwellings and even a housing project are close by, but some fabulous Depression-era artwork (lower right) brightens the neighborhood.

A large hunk of the new, diamond-shaped District of Columbia above Florida Avenue, then called "Boundary Street," was not even detailed in Pierre L'Enfant's original Plan for Washington. It was an empty glen that was simply called "Washington County." But after the Civil War, fashionable Washington began to push northward along once-rustic Thirteenth Street (opposite) and Sixteenth Street (lower left). The latter became the city's first Embassy Row, lined with fine mansions. Richardsonian and Victorian townhouses spread up Thirteenth from what became Logan Circle (top left). It was named for Civil War General John Logan—who came up with the idea for Memorial Day— even though Logan, as a U.S. Senator from Illinois, tried to get the nation's capital moved to Saint Louis.

Adams-Morgan (top right) has become a magnet for Washington's exploding Hispanic population, though its writers' garrets and little restaurants and shops retain a SoHo flavor. The neighborhood, once called Lanier Heights, got its new name after Washington desegregated its schools in the 1950s—Adams had been an all-white school, Morgan all black. A tribute to Washington native Duke Ellington (lower left) decorates the revitalized Shaw neighborhood, once the locus of African-American culture and nightlife. U Street, where Ellington, Louis Armstrong, and other legends performed, was known as "Black Broadway." One of the newest Metro stops, the restored Lincoln Theater, and esoteric eateries like Ben's Chili Bowl (opposite) surround it. On Massachusetts Avenue is another mural to a legendary African American: Frederick Douglass (lower right).

Washington's China-town neighborhood, largely confined to H Street and minuscule by New York or San Francisco standards, is nonetheless colorful. There had been other Chinese enclaves, notably one within a block of the U.S. Capitol, but each had been rousted by one development project after another. Chinatown presents a veritable groaning board of restaurants, which gained renewed popularity among Washington visitors in the late 1990s when the city's giant MCI sports arena opened on its doorstep. Even though relations between the United States and China have often been strained, their capital cities have maintained a warm sister-city relationship. In 1986, Beijing presented Wash-ington with a Qing Dynasty-style "Friend-ship Arch" (far right), which architect Alfred Liu said imitated "the diversity of life itself."

In most nations, embassies are utilitarian places established for the paperwork of state. Few visitors pay much attention to ambassadors' homes or the splendor of chanceries. But in Washington, embassies connote off-limits mansions where elegant dinners are spread; theme parties thrown; dinner jackets, lavish gowns, and precious gems paraded; fine wines tested; exotic tongues spoken; and fabulous furnishings savored. The Indonesian Embassy (left), on Massachusetts Avenue's "Embassy Row," was built in 1903 by Tom Walsh, a miner who had struck gold near Ouray, Colorado. Inside today, marble dancers on the Y-shaped grand staircase beckon to a promenade gallery leading to second-floor suites. American-born architect Masao Kinoshita designed the Japanese ambassador's home (opposite). The house, garden, and teahouse were dedicated in 1979.

The house of the Belgian ambassador (top left) replicates the Hôtel de Charolais in Paris. Distiller Thomas Gaff incorporated conveniences like a hot-air clothes-drying system into the house (top right) that became the Colombian ambassador's residence. In *Father Struck it Rich*, Evelyn Walsh McLean described life in the house that is now the Indonesian Embassy (center left). The widow of the builder of the Brooklyn Bridge commissioned Villa Firenze (center right)—which today is the Italian Embassy. Across the street from Woodrow Wilson's house, his brother-in-law built what is now the residence of the Dutch ambassador (lower left). Architect George Oakley Totten was told "cost is no object" for the house that evolved into the home of the Turkish ambassador (lower right). Intrigue filled the French Embassy (opposite) during the World War II Vichy period.

The Spanish ambassador's patio (opposite) is an imitation of an Andalusian courtyard. Inside the Ecuadorian ambassador's residence is a colonial wooden chest featuring iron chains, brass bells, and a statue of the "Apocalyptic" Virgin (top left). In the "Seduction Room"—as visitors have dubbed it—of the Kuwaiti Embassy, gold brocade lines the niches of the carved Arabesque paneling (center left). Behind an entrance hall statue in the home of the Luxembourg ambassador (lower left), the stairway's carved balustrade depicts flora and fauna. A vase adds color to the sunroom of the Turkish Embassy (top right). A statue of the Mahatma, Mohandas Karamchand Gandhi, sits outside the Indian ambassador's office (center right). The music room of the Mexican Cultural Institute (lower right) features a full-scale pipe organ and a Louis XIII-style chair.

Diplomats enjoy some of Washington's prime gardens. One such green space at the British Embassy is the site of some of Washington's most coveted diplomatic parties (far right). In another of its greenswards stands a bronze statue of Sir Winston Churchill, flashing his "V for Victory" sign with one hand and clutching a prodigious cigar in the other. The gardens of the Dutch Embassy (top right) were once the pride of "traction baron" Charles Owsley, who ran a Chicago "el" line but moved his family to Washington. At the residence of the Danish ambassador, a wall of ceramic birds native to Denmark (center right) embellishes an open area. A marble fountain in a courtyard of the Apostolic Nunciature of the Holy See— or Vatican Embassy— (lower right) copies a larger one in Rome.